BRANCH LINES AROUND SPALDING

Michael Back

Series editor Vic Mitchell

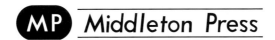

MP Middleton Press

Front cover: The last up Yarmouth to Birmingham express is ready to leave Spalding, the inward service having been drawn forward and backed into the Bourne Line, platform 7. The headboard went through to Leicester and returned later in the day on the down working. (J.Langford)

Back cover upper: Another last day, this time the final up morning goods train to call at Gedney. It is 1st February 1964, the last day that the station was open; the signal box closed a fortnight later and the loop was taken out of use. The porter wheels away the last few parcels, while the closure notice is outside the door.

Back cover lower: An up LNWR express passes Fleet in around 1925, its first year of running. It appears to be hauled by one of the large-boilered 4-4-0s. All is immaculate on the platform and the goods yard is full of vans. This train ran from Yarmouth to Liverpool via Manchester.

Published 50 years after the closure of the M&GN.

Published May 2009

ISBN 978 1 906008 52 9

© *Middleton Press, 2009*

Design Deborah Esher
Typesetting Barbara Mitchell

Published by
        Middleton Press
        Easebourne Lane
        Midhurst
        West Sussex
        GU29 9AZ
Tel: 01730 813169
Fax: 01730 812601
Email: info@middletonpress.co.uk
www.middletonpress.co.uk

Printed in the United Kingdom by Henry Ling Limited, at the Dorset Press, Dorchester, DT1 1HD

INDEX

ACKNOWLEDGEMENTS

R.Adderson, D.Brown, M.Clark, G.Croughton, F.Gent, G.Gosling, L.Hails, M.Hodge, G.Kenworthy, J.Langford, N.Langridge, V.Mitchell, M&GN Circle Photo Archive, J.Newell, V.Simpson, D.F.Smith, D.Soggee, R.Watson, plus Mrs J.Back without who nothing would be possible. Mention should also be made of the late E.L.Back MBE. All photographs, unless otherwise credited, are from his camera; he was the father of the author.

I. Plan showing the route in 1958. (Railway Magazine)

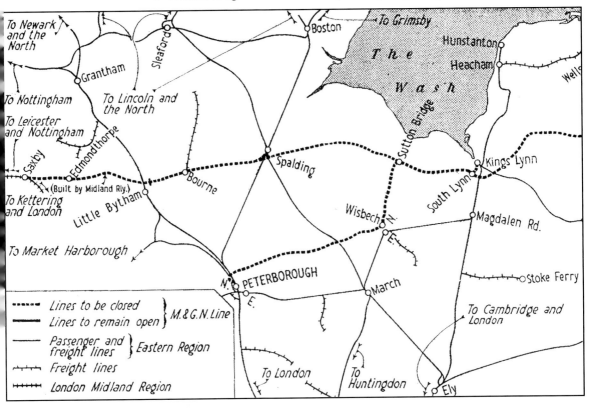

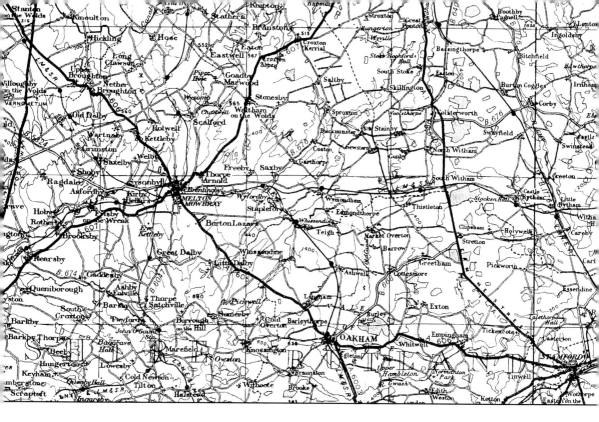

GEOGRAPHICAL SETTING

The undulating pastures and uplands to the east of Melton Mowbray are deceptive and the line alternates between embankments and shallow cuttings to avoid severe gradients. Approaching South Witham, there are ironstone deposits just to the north and other quarries produced limestone. This terrain culminates in the deep rock cuttings at Castle Bytham, before reaching the valley of the West Glen River. The main line to the north also utilises this valley on its climb to Stoke Summit and the single track crosses over this at Little Bytham Junction.

Continuing from here as double track, the long defunct course of the Edenham Railway is also crossed, this having fallen out of use as early as 1866. There are then deeper cuttings, the sides of which posed problems and speed restrictions for many years, before crossing the East Glen River over the Lound viaduct. Then comes Toft Tunnel, 15 chains in length, often said to be the only one on the M&GN, although there is a much shorter one near Cromer.

This is the end of the higher ground. Approaching Bourne are clay deposits near the line and a small brick and tile industry flourished here around the turn of the last century. From Bourne onwards the line runs across the flat Fen area, climbing slightly to cross several drainage channels en route to Spalding. The soils are the most fertile in eastern England and huge crops are grown, most of which were once despatched by rail. The area was prone to flooding, especially around Spalding where the Washes were once full of water, but in later days fewer problems were encountered. →

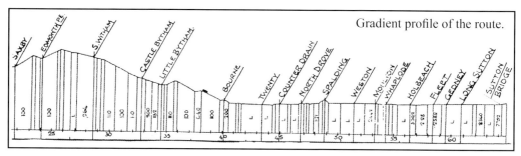

Gradient profile of the route.

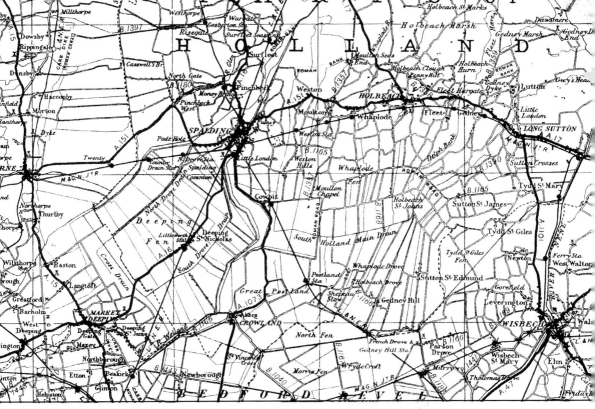

The former Fen rivers have now silted up and been reduced to mere dykes. Having climbed round the Spalding avoiding line and the River Welland, the line is once again flat all the way to the junction with the Peterborough to Lynn line at Sutton Bridge.

Maps are to the scale of 9 inches to the mile unless otherwise indicated, with north at the top.

II.   Map of the area at ¼ ins to 1 mile. Our route branches off from the Midland Railway at Saxby. It crosses the Great Northern Railway main line on an overbridge at Little Bytham, where the M&GN began at an end-on junction. On the right page is Bourne where the GNR line from Essendine to Sleaford briefly joins our route. The line then reaches Spalding. Continuing across the flat Fen area the line runs to Holbeach, the first temporary terminus on this part of the route. The line joins the Peterborough to South Lynn line at Sutton Bridge.

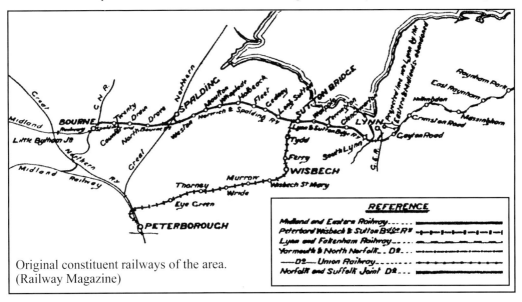

Original constituent railways of the area.
(Railway Magazine)

HISTORICAL BACKGROUND

The history of the lines in this book is far from easy to unravel, and there were many Acts of Parliament. The line from Spalding, as far as Holbeach, opened for goods on 28th July 1858 and for passengers on 15th November 1858. By agreement, the Great Northern Railway undertook to work the line. Delays required a further Act of 13th August 1859 and the line was opened to Sutton Bridge on 3rd July 1862.

Next was the Spalding & Bourne Railway, which was empowered under its Act of 29th July 1862. This was to join the GNR's line from Essendine at an end-on junction at Bourn. (Mostly spelt without the 'e' until 1894). This line opened on 1st August 1866. However, by the somewhat complicated Act of 23rd July 1866, the Midland & Eastern Railway was formed. This amalgamated the Spalding & Bourne and the neighbouring Lynn & Sutton Bridge and was to lease the Norwich & Spalding. This arrangement actually came into being under a prior agreement of 6th July 1866 and, confusingly, was operated jointly by the Great Northern and the Midland Railway under the title of Bourn & Lynn Committee. The GNR was to maintain the whole line from Bourn to Sutton Bridge.

An Act of 18th August 1882 then formed the Eastern & Midland Railway, which was to amalgamate with the local lines in Norfolk. This came into being on 1st July 1883 and also absorbed the Midland & Eastern Railway. Thus the scene was set for the formation of the Midland & Great Northern Joint Committee on 1st July 1893, owned jointly by these two companies.

All this time the Midland Railway had also been keenly interested in the line west of Bourn and there had been proposals, as far back as 1866, to extend the new line from Spalding through to Saxby or even Cottesmore, on the Midland Railway. Finally, an Act of 24th June 1889 authorised a line from Saxby to Bourn and the MR commenced construction. A further Act of 25th July 1890 authorised a loop at Spalding, the avoiding line, which also included its connecting spurs from west and east into Spalding GNR station. Heavy earthworks were necessary for these and both new lines opened for goods traffic on 5th June 1893 and for passengers on 1st May 1894. A new station at Bourn opened on 23rd June 1893. Although not within the scope of this book, the original line from Essendine then became the branch. There was also a line northwards from Bourn to Sleaford which had opened to goods on 10th September 1871 and for passengers on 2nd January 1872.

Few changes occurred for many years. At Bourne the Sleaford line was closed to passengers on 22nd September 1930 and the Essendine branch closed completely on 18th June 1951. The M&GN line lost its passenger service on 28th February 1959. Spalding to Bourne and from there to Billingborough on the Sleaford line, was worked as one long siding with one train working out in the morning and back in the afternoon. Bourne to South Witham was closed completely. Spalding to Sutton Bridge retained a fairly good service of two trains down and three trains back, almost until the final closure and for a while traffic increased. Both lines closed completely on 4th April 1965. Saxby to South Witham had remained open for freight after 1959, mainly for ironstone, but this part of the route closed in 1966.

PASSENGER SERVICES

In reviewing these services it must be remembered that the two original companies, the Spalding & Bourne and the Norwich & Spalding, both worked separate trains on their lines. The former ran through to Essendine, although this is outside the scope of this book. On 6th January 1869 there were just three trains each way on that line. On the Spalding to Sutton Bridge line there were four trains each way, the last up train terminating at Holbeach. Not all trains called at all stations, the smaller ones were by request. Moving on to February 1890, there were now four trains each way on the Bourne & Spalding line, the first from Bourne having the distinction of a slip-coach from London. This must have entailed some smart working at Essendine, where there were no direct track connections between the line from Bourne and the GNR branch to Stamford and Wansford. The Spalding to Sutton Bridge line had five trains each way, all of which started or terminated at Kings Lynn. There was an extra down train on Saturdays and on Tuesdays an extra up train with limited stops.

The timetable of December 1895 shows quite a change, as trains ran through from Saxby on the new line recently opened. Essendine has now disappeared. There were six trains each way between Bourne and Spalding, with three being to or from Saxby. There was a pattern of Saxby line services only calling to pick up or set down at stations between Bourne and Spalding, worked by the Midland Railway, with GNR trains to Bourne providing the service at those intermediate stations. Spalding and Sutton Bridge had five trains each way, with the extras on Saturdays and Tuesdays previously mentioned.

These services set the pattern for several years. In July 1910 we see the famous express, known as *The Leicester*. This did not stop between Bourne and South Lynn in the east, using the Spalding avoiding line. In fact, in the timetable for November 1930, these trains, one in each direction, are shown as being through carriages, Gloucester, Birmingham and Leicester to Sheringham, Norwich, Yarmouth and Lowestoft.

Moving forward to almost the last timetable of August 1958, we see the regional demarcation as Saxby to Bourne appears in a separate table, even though some trains are shown in both to be through services. There were still only the three trains a day for the intermediate stations. There were four trains each way between Bourne and Spalding. From there to Sutton Bridge there were six down and five up trains, calling at most stations. An addition was the Leicester express, which from 18th September 1955 had been routed into Spalding.

A large number of summer dated trains were run. These were supplemented by numerous excursions, which made the former M&GN line one of the most extensively worked single lines on Summer Saturdays. Your author travelled on the 8.0am train from Sutton Bridge to Spalding and the 4.0pm back at this time, as these were the school trains; three old carriages packed to capacity! Memories remain of the 4.0pm home racing the 4.0pm to Saxby from the opposite side of Spalding station. The latter was then, it seems, worked by Midland men and the old rivalries still seemed to exist.

June 1869

STAMFORD, ESSENDINE, BOURNE, SPALDING, HOLBEACH, SUTTON BRIDGE, and LYNN.—Great Northern.

December 1895

PETERBRO', BOURNE, SPALDING, SUTTON BRIDGE, and LYNN.—Mid. & G. N. Joint.

Down.

Fares from Peterbro'.				Station											
1 cl.	3 cl.	RETURN		232 LONDON (K.C.) dep.	5 15		7 15		1015	1 30	3 0		3 0	5 0	
0 9	0 4	1 6 0 8		Peterbro' (G. E.)..dep.			9 12		1140	3 0				6 55	
1 3	0 7	2 6 1 2		" (Gt. North.) "	6 55		9 20		1153	3 6	4 40		4 48	7 5	
1 7	0 9	3 2 1 6		Eye Green	7 6		9 31		12 4	3 17			4 59	7 16	
2 0	1 1	4 0 2 1		Thorney	7 13		9 39		1212	3 24			5 7	7 23	
2 6	1 4	5 0 2 8		Wryde			9 43		12 6	3 29			5 13	7 29	
2 9	1 6	5 6 3 1		Murrow 246, 216	7 24		9 51		1221	3 37			5 22	7 38	
3 2	1 9	6 4 3 6		Wisbech St. Mary	Sig.		9 57		1230	3 44			5 28	7 45	
3 5	1 11	6 10 3 10		Wisbech * 176	7 36		10 4		1236	3 52	5 12		5 34	7 51	
3 10	2 1	7 8 4 3		Ferry			10 9		1241	3 58				7 57	
				Tydd			1014		1246	4 4				8 3	
				Sutton Bridge ....arr.	7 49		1020		1251	4 9	5 24			8 8	
				401 BIRMINGHAM † dep.			7 50		11 5			3 k 0		4 50	
				LEICESTER 391 "		7k25	9 35		1250			4k35		6 25	
2 6	1 6½			Saxby ....dep.			1028		1 37					7 33	
2 11	1 10	5 10 3 8		Edmondthorpe ‡			1034		1 43					7 39	
2 9	1 8½	5 6 3 5		South Witham			1042		1 51					7 47	
2 6	1 7	5 0 3 2		Bourne 231, 230	7 55		1050 1113		2 27				6 5	8 18	
				Twenty	8 2		1057		2 34				6 13		
2 3	1 4½			Counter Drain	8 6		11 2		Sig.				6 17		
				North Drove	8 9		11 7		Sig.				6 22		
2 6	1 7	5 0 3 2		Spalding 216, { arr.	8 16		1115 1133		2 49				6 29	8 37	
2 11	1 10	5 10 3 8		246 { dep.	8 38	9 30			1140	3 5	5 35		8 20		
3 2	2 0	6 4 4 0		Weston	8 45	9 36			1146	3 12	5 41		Sig.		
3 5	2 2	6 10 4 4		Moulton	8 49	9 40			1150	3 17	5 48		8 30		
3 8	2 3½	7 4 4 7		Whaplode	8 52	9 43			1153	3 20	5 48		8 34		
3 8	2 4	7 4 4 8		Holbeach	8 59	9 50			12 0	3 26	5 55		8 41		
				Fleet	9 4	9 54			12 4	3 31	6 0		8 46		
				Gedney	9 8	9 57			12 8	3 35	6 4		8 50		
				Long Sutton	9 12	10 1			1212	3 39	6 7		8 54		
				Sutton Bridge arr.	9 20	1010			1218	3 46	6 10		9 2		
4 1	2 4½	3 2 4 9		Sutton Bridge...dep.	7 50	9 23	1022		1222	1252	1 10	5 25	6 20	8 4	9 5
4 4	2 6½	8 8 5 1		Walpole		9 27	1028		1228		h	Sig.	6 27	8 16	d
4 8	2 8	9 4 5 4		Terrington	7 59	9 32	1033		1233		h	4 19	6 33	8 22	9 14
				Clenchwarton	8 3	9 36	1037		1237		h	Sig.	b		
4 11	2 10	9 10 5 8		South Lynn 218	8 10	9 42	1044		1244		1 12	4 27	5 40	6 43	8 30 9 23
				218 NORWICH § ....arr.	1030		1252		3 20		3 20	7 58	7 58		
13 5	7 3	24 4 1310		218 YARMOUTH ‖..arr.	1125	1 45	1 45				8 44	8 44			
4 11	2 10	9 10 5 8		Lynn 176, 177 ..arr.	8 18	9 52	1052		1252		1 20	4 35	5 50	6 52	8 38 9 30

Up.

Fares.				Station			mrn	mrn	mrn		mrn	aft	aft	aft	aft	aft	aft
SINGLE.		RETURN		Lynn ....dep.	7 5	8 30		9 50			1155	1 5	2 10	3 40	4 53	5 45	6 58
1 cl.	3 cl.	1 cl.	3 cl.	219 YARMOUTH ‖..dep.				7 0						1 50		1 50	
s. d.	s. d.	s. d.	s. d.	NORWICH §219 "				7 55						2 55		2 55	
0 4	0 2	0 8	0 4	South Lynn	7 10	8 35		10 5			12 0	1 14	2 15	3 45	5 5	5 52	7 3
0 8	0 5	1 4	0 10	Clenchwarton	7 17	Sig.		Sig.			Sig.	Sig.	f	3 52		5 59	Sig.
0 11	0 6	1 10	1 0	Terrington	7 22	8 45		1013			1210	1 25	2 24	3 56		6 3	7 11
1 3	0 8	2 6	1 4	Walpole	7 27	8 50					Sig.	1 30		4 1		6 8	Sig.
1 6	0 11	3 0	1 10	Sutton Bridge.... arr.	7 33	8 56		1021			1220	1 35	2 32	4 8	5 22	6 14	7 19
2 0	1 2½	4 0	2 5	Sutton Bridge...dep.	7 34	9 25		1030			1 36			4 12			7 20
2 2	1 3½	4 4	2 7	Long Sutton	7 41	9 32		1037			1 43			4 18			7 27
2 4	1 5	4 8	2 10	Gedney	Sig.	9 36		1040			1 46			4 21			7 31
2 7	1 7	5 2	3 2	Fleet	Sig.	9 40		1044			1 50			4 25			7 35
2 10	1 9	5 8	3 6	Holbeach	7 54	9 45		1050			1 56			4 31			7 42
2 11	1 10	5 10	3 8	Whaplode	Sig.	9 50		1056			2 2			4 35			Sig.
3 3	1 11½	6 6	3 11	Moulton	8 3	9 54		11 0			2 6			4 39			7 51
3 4	2 0½	6 8	4 1	Weston	Sig.	9 58		Sig.			Sig.			4 44			7 55
				Spalding 216, { arr.	8 15	10 5		11 5			2 16			4 48			8 0
3 10	2 4½	7 8	4 9	246 { dep.	8 38	9 5					1145		2 58	4 56	5 30		
				North Drove	Sig.						1151			c	5 36		
4 7	2 10	9 2	5 8	Counter Drain	Sig.						1155			c	5 40		
6 1	3 9	12 2	7 7	Twenty	8 53						1159			c	5 45		
6 9	4 2	13 6	8 4	Bourne 231, 230	9 0	9 29					12 7		3 21	5 22	5 52		
7 0	4 4½	14 0	8 9	South Witham		9 49					1235			5 42			
				Edmondthorpe ‡	Stop	10 1					1247			5 54			
9 7	5 10½	19 2	11 9	Saxby 391, 392..arr.		10 7					1253			6 0			
1410	9 1	29 8	18 2	LEICESTER 391 arr.		1116	12k2				1 44			6 50			9k40
				396 BIRMINGHAM † "		1250	3 k 0				3 0			8 25			12 k7
1 10	1 1½	3 8	2 3	Sutton Bridge....dep.		8 57		1022			1 22	2 33		5 23			6 20
2 2	1 3½	4 4	2 7	Tydd		9 3					Sig.	2 39					6 26
2 3	1 3½	4 5	2 6	Ferry	mrn	9 8					i	2 45					6 32
2 9	1 5½	5 2	11	Wisbech * 176	8 5	9 15		1034			1237	2 53		5 36	5 50		6 41
3 2	1 9	6 4	3 6	Wisbech St. Mary	8 10	9 20					Sig.	2 59			5 56		6 47
3 8	2 1	7 4	4 2	Murrow 246, 216	8 17	9 27					1250	3 6			6 2		6 54
4 0	2 3	8 0	4 6	Wryde	8 21	9 34					Sig.	3 13					7 1
4 6	2 6	9 0	5 0	Thorney ....{391, 246	8 29	9 39		1051			1 1	3 23					7 6
4 11	2 10	9 10	5 8	Eye Green..{244, 232,	8 37	9 48		11 1			1 9	3 31		g			7 15
				Peterbro' (G.N.) 237,	8 46	9 58		1114			1 20	3 46			6 7		7 25
				" (G. E.) 290		10 2											7 30
15 0	8 0½	27 2	16 1	237 LONDON (K.C.) arr.	11e9		1145			1 5		3 25	5 45		8 5		9 20

BOURNE, SPALDING (Town), HOLBEACH, SUTTON BRIDGE and KING'S LYNN

MONDAYS TO FRIDAYS

Miles		am	am	am	pm		pm	pm		pm	pm
—	**Bourne** dep	7 40	10 37	..	..	Lon. Rd.) to	4 24	..	(Table 50)	5 59	9 19
3¾	Twenty	7 47	10 44	..	..			..		6 6	9 26
5¼	Counter Drain	7 51	10 48	..	..			..		6 10	9 30
7¼	North Drove	7 55	10 52	..	..			..		6 14	9 34
9¾	**Spalding (Town)** arr	8 0	10 57	..	..		4 39	..	Lynn	6 19	9 39
24¼	54 Boston arr	11K25	12 58	..	..	Leicester (New St.) and	6 11	..	King's	7 17	....
26¼	54 Peterborough (N'th) arr	8 42	12 47	..	..		5 33	..	to	7 55	8 10 32
102½	54 London (King's C.) ,,	10 38	3 35	..	..		7 56	..		9 38	2₀55
—	54 London (King's C.) dep	4 0	8 20	..	1 20		..	2 10	Midland)	4 15	..
—	54 Peterborough (N'th) ,,	6 25	10 10	..	3 0		..	5 3		5 52	..
—	54 Boston dep	7 31	10 10	11 40	2 9		..	5 12		5 12	..
—	**Spalding (Town)** dep	8 15	11 23	12 20	4 0		4 46	5 57		6 50	....
12	Weston	8 23		11 34	12 24	4 8				7 0	
13½	Moulton	8 30		11 34	12 30	4 12		6 7	7 0	
14½	Whaplode	8 33		11 38	12 33	4 15		6 10	7 3	
17	Holbeach	8 39		11 49	12 38	4 20		6 15	7 8	
19	Fleet	8 44		11 54	12 43	4 25			7 13	
20½	Gedney	8 48		11 58	12 47	4 29		6 22	7 17	
21½	Long Sutton	8 51		12 1	12 51	4 32		6 25	7 20	
25½	Sutton Bridge arr	8 58		12 8	12 58	4 39		6 32	7 27	
34½	South Lynn ,,	9 19		12 29	2 30	5 3	5 23	7A12	7 47	
36½	King's Lynn ,,	9 25		12 36	2 41	5 10	5 34	6 52	7 53	

SATURDAYS ONLY

am	am	am	am	am	am	am
7 40	8 29	(Beach)	9 13	10 23	10 37	11 9
7 47					10 44	
7 51					10 48	
7 55					10 52	
8 0					10 57	
		Cromer			11 43	
8 42					11F50	
10 38					1F27	
4 0						
6 25						
7 31						
8 15						
8 23						
8 30						
8 33						
8 39						
8 44						
8 48						
8 51						
8 58						
9 19	9 38		10 13	11 22		12 22
9 25	9 55		10 29	11 37		12 55

SATURDAYS ONLY—continued

	am	am	pm		pm	am	pm		pm	pm	pm	pm
Bourne dep	..	11 34	12 2		12 24	..	2 13	..		4 24	4 35	..	5 57	9 19
Twenty	....					....	2 20	..			4 42	....	6 6	9 26
Counter Drain	..					....	2 24	..			4 46	....	6 10	9 30
North Drove	....					....	2 28	..			4 50	....	6 14	9 34
Spalding (Town) arr	..					....	2 33	..			4 55	....	6 19	9 39
54 Boston arr	..					....	3 10	..			5 55	....	7 17	....
54 Peterborough (N'th) arr	..					....	3 19	..			6 13	....	7 5	10 32
54 London (King's C.) ,,	..					....	5 4	..			8 9	....	10T 2	2₀55
54 London (King's C.) dep	..	9 18				....	..	1 18			3 0	4 8	..	..
54 Peterborough (N'th) ,,	..	10 57				....	..	3 0			4 45	5 46	..	..
54 Boston dep	11 6				11 40	..	2 23			5 14	5 38	..	..
Spalding (Town) dep	11 43				12 32	..	4 0			..	5 57	6 50	..
Weston						12 43	4 8				6 7	7 0	..
Moulton	11 57				12 43	4 12				6 10	7 3	..	10 50
Whaplode	12 0				12 46	4 15				6 15	7 8	..	10 59
Holbeach	12 8				12 54	4 20					7 13	..	
Fleet	12 13				12 59	4 25					7 17	..	
Gedney	12 17				1 6	4 29				6 22	7 20	..	
Long Sutton	12 20				1 13	4 32				6 25	7 24	..	
Sutton Bridge arr	12 27				1 49	2 15	4 39			6 32	7 27	..	
South Lynn ,,	12 48	12 54	1 9		2 35	5 3			5 21	7A12	7 47	..	11 40
King's Lynn ,,	12 55	1C10	1 25		2 35	5 10			5 34	6 52	7 54	..	

SUNDAYS

am	am
10 22	..
10 30	..
10 34	..
10 38	..
..	..
..	..
..	7 45
..	10 15
..	10 53
..	11 4
..	11 7
..	11 16
..	11 20
..	11 23
..	..
11 40	11 50

A Change at Sutton Bridge
a am
C Runs 12th July to 30th August inclusive

F On 14th and 21st June arr Peterborough (North) 12 8 and King's Cross 1 50 pm
K On Thursdays 17th July to 28th August inclusive arr Boston 11 11 am

RB Buffet Car
T From 19th July to 30th August arr King's Cross 9 10 pm
TC Through Carriages

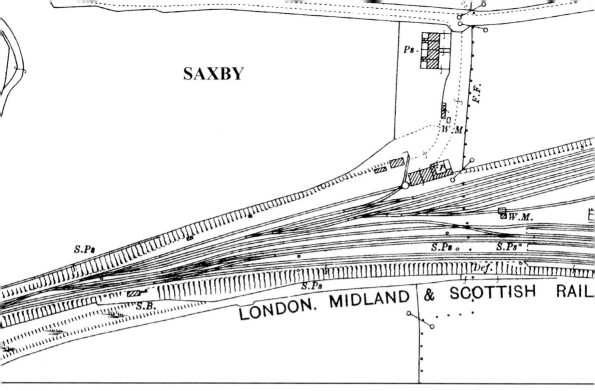

SAXBY

III.   This was a busy junction, Saxby West Junction signal box being on the left. On the right of this 1930 plan there is a wealth of history, the "Old Railway" at the top being "Lord Harborough's Curve". He was the local landowner and objected very strongly to the Midland Railway being routed from Melton Mowbray through his grounds of Stapleford Park. He and his employees met the railway staff in the "Battle of Saxby", when the latter were evicted by force. Eventually the →

1.   Class 4MT no. 43063 runs in with a train for the Spalding line, sometime in the early 1950s. The stock is typical for that era. (M&GN Circle Photo Archive)

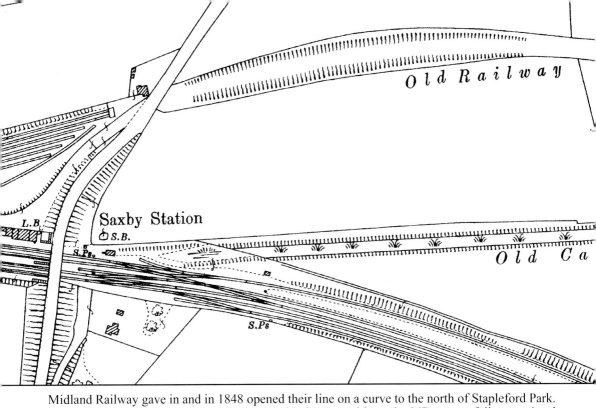

Old Railway

Saxby Station

L.B.

S.B.

S.Ps.

Old Ca

S.Ps

Midland Railway gave in and in 1848 opened their line on a curve to the north of Stapleford Park. The speed restriction this necessitated was a hindrance and later the MR successfully negotiated with Lord Harborough's successor to re-route their line as first proposed. This and a new station opened on 28th August 1892, the old line and level crossing being closed: the two routes met further east at Wymondham Goods Junction. The scale is 25ins to 1 mile.

2.   The start of the line towards Bourne, seen from a passing train on the main line on 4th June 1960. The single line facing points are in the centre, and over on the left is the long disused site of Lord Harborough's curve.

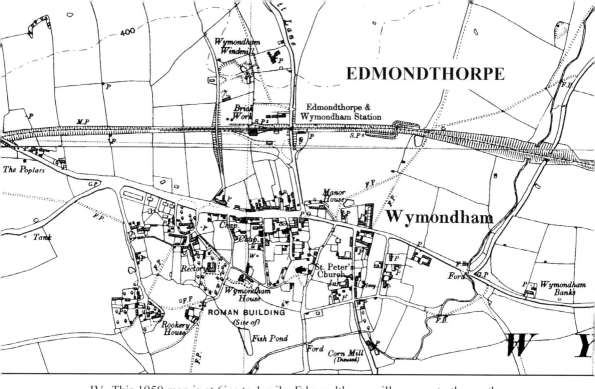

IV. This 1950 map is at 6ins to 1 mile. Edmondthorpe village was to the south.

3.　　Seen in February 1959 is the up side station building and signal box, a Midland Railway type built on a brick lower storey. The crossing loop was extended on 13th April 1941 to accommodate wartime trains; there was then a very heavy traffic along the line for the numerous airfields in East Anglia. (L.Hails)

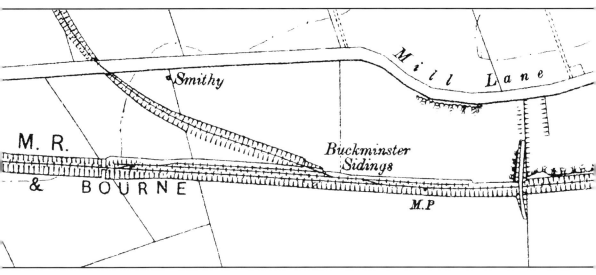

V.   Mainstay of the freight traffic along this part of the line was the ironstone quarried from several sites, first at Pain's Siding and a short distance further at Buckminster. This 1931 map is at 12ins to 1 mile and the branch to the north serves not only the mine of that name but continued to join up with the GNR line from Highdyke to Stainby.

SOUTH WITHAM

4.   This station has wooden platforms, being on an embankment. The view is looking towards Bourne in early 1959. The goods yard and signal box are behind the photographer. (L.Hails)

VI. Also from 1931, at 12ins to 1 mile, this shows the quarry near the station.

5.   Lifting the track near South Witham began in the middle of the 1960s. This was removed in the direction of Saxby and the track panels taken out by train, probably to go to Beeston. The flat countryside looks rather like the area around Buckminster Sidings.

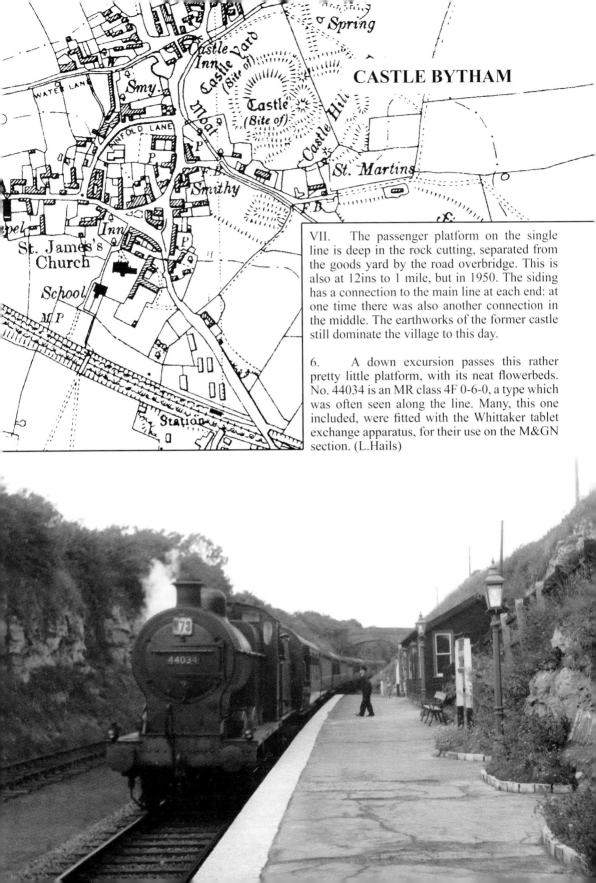

CASTLE BYTHAM

VII.   The passenger platform on the single line is deep in the rock cutting, separated from the goods yard by the road overbridge. This is also at 12ins to 1 mile, but in 1950. The siding has a connection to the main line at each end: at one time there was also another connection in the middle. The earthworks of the former castle still dominate the village to this day.

6.   A down excursion passes this rather pretty little platform, with its neat flowerbeds. No. 44034 is an MR class 4F 0-6-0, a type which was often seen along the line. Many, this one included, were fitted with the Whittaker tablet exchange apparatus, for their use on the M&GN section. (L.Hails)

7.   We look down on the platform from the high overbridge at the Bourne end of the station as an up train has just passed. Access from the road is down the long slope on the right. On the left is the west end of the goods siding, which extends behind the photographer. Access is by tablet-released ground frames at each end: the cabin containing the one at the west end can be seen near the end of the train. (L.Hails)

8.   Having crossed over the GNR main line, we come to the end-on junction between the MR and the M&GN, which was marked by a special boundary post on each side of the line. As these faced each other, one was the reverse; this is the up side post, still in situ on 18th May 1959, with the line from Saxby on which we have travelled on the right.

9.　　　This MR type signal box was at the junction, where the single line became double towards the east. Taken around 1957, there appears to be ample coal for the signal box stove. The more modern WC cubicle is on the far side of the box, and the tablet catcher is in front of it. On the left is a cowhorn tablet receiver, illuminated by a lamp, for engines not equipped with the Whittaker apparatus.

WEST OF BOURNE

10.　　　Looking through Toft Tunnel, from the Bourne end, in May 1960, the shallowness of the overburden is noticeable, in fact a cutting here would have been less deep than some of the cuttings on the line to the west. In the M&GN numbering sequence, this was Bridge no. 237.

St. Peter's
Pool

BOURNE

Bourne Eau

F.B.

Cor
Mil

• Spring
Watercress
Beds

Red Hall

F.B.

S.P

Tk.

S.P

W.M.

Stat

F.P.

M.P.

S.Ps

S.B.

F.P.

S.P

S.P

S.P

Tk.

F.P.

F.P.

F.B.

HERN JOINT RAILWAY

S.P.

F.P.

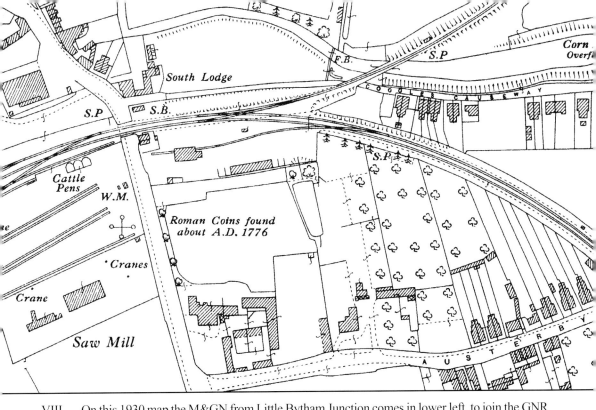

VIII.   On this 1930 map the M&GN from Little Bytham Junction comes in lower left, to join the GNR lines from Essendine coming in from the south. Ths siding shown before the footbridge is reached is Kingston's Siding, which served a brick and tile works. After traffic ceased, it was converted into a down refuge siding. The scale is 25ins to 1 mile.

11.   Proof that Midland Railway engines used the shed is here, with the resplendent class 1P 4-4-0 no. 323 posing outside in all its glory. Express headlamps are mounted, and it is ready to take over Special no. 300 back to the Midlands but the date is unknown.

12.   We examine the west end of the station and Bourne West signal box. We are standing on the former main line to Saxby; the site of the branch to Essendine on the right has had the goods yard spur slewed over into it. A Barclay diesel shunter and its train stand in the platform. On the left is the old loco shed and the goods shed is on the right. This is 17th August 1960 and the signal box is not in use, all points being worked by hand.

13.   We look back from the platform in the last summer of passenger services, 1958, with the line to Saxby curving sharply round to the right where once there were brick and tile works in the distance. These had been controlled by a separate signal box named Kingston's Siding. The fine water column is still in daily use and the siding on the left is the shunt spur, on the site of the old Essendine line. The junction for this has been taken out, and the lefthand arm of the bracket signal removed. We note the lamp case on its post. The brick cabin on the right of the signal box was once used by the Railway Clearing House numbertakers. As at most junctions between different lines, they were stationed here to count the number of wagons exchanged between the railway companies. (L.Hails)

14.   The station is seen from the west box. A 4MT locomotive is shunting in the goods yard in the centre, next to the large goods shed. In the distance can just be seen the East signal box. (L.Hails)

15.   Another LMS 4F 0-6-0 is about to leave with Special no. 104 and looking much cleaner than these predominantly freight locos often were. Ivatt 2-6-0 class 4MT is waiting on the right, sometime in September 1958. (D.Soggee)

16.   The Permanent Way department at Bourne had one of the delightful little motorised trolleys and here we see M&GN Rail Motor no. 3 outside its shed in the goods yard. The author and his father visited on 17th August 1960 and the driver seen here obligingly pulled it out for us. Its fate is not known.

17.   The large 2-road GNR engine shed was extended in length in 1898. Behind this on 17th August 1960 is the tall water tower. Motive power for the Sleaford and Essendine lines came from here, and Midland Railway engines used it by agreement. It was run down in the 1930s and finally closed when its remaining duties were transferred to Spalding around 1950.

18.   Ivatt 2-6-0 no. 43058 has an admirer, whilst it waits to take a stopping train out to the west. Another passenger train pauses in the down platform. The very nice lamp is without its vessel; often these were cleaned and filled during the day and returned at dusk. (L.Hails)

19.   The loco shed is on the right. The original turntable of 45ft was changed for one of 60ft in 1930. The goods shed is larger than normal. The signal is Bourne East down home; the replacement arm is on a concrete post.

20.   Barclay 204hp 0-6-0 diesel loco no. 1178 waits in the goods yard on 17th August 1960: it has the "lion on a wheel" crest above the number on the cab side. Whilst these engines were not powerful enough for the line to Sutton Bridge, they were adequate for the lesser loadings on the Bourne line after 1959.

21.   No coverage of Bourne would be complete without the Red Hall, of Elizabethan origin. The GNR wanted to demolish the old Hall, but fortunately were persuaded not to do so. The platform of the original station was where the railings are and for a while the Hall was used as the booking office. On the left is the down side water column and the hut on the right is the booking office, used up to closure. The date is 17th August 1960.

22.   The East junction is seen on the same day with the line to Sleaford on the left and to Spalding on the right. Since 2nd March 1959, the line throughout has been worked as a siding from Spalding and so the only track in use is the former up main, on the right. The track on the left now only leads towards Billingborough, the line beyond there to Sleaford having been closed. Both the junction facing and trailing points are clamped for those respective directions and beyond there the old down main is being removed. The M&GN had a separate goods yard and this is the siding on the right; the long building is the old stables and offices.

23.   Just round the corner is the neat little Austerby box and it is seen on 17th August 1960 from the footbridge, which had to be provided at the insistence of the Board of Trade. The gates are chained and padlocked. As with most other crossings along the line, these were opened and closed by the train crew. This took so long that the daily freight managed to get to Bourne, reverse and then arrive at Billingborough before the crew had to be relieved! A second crew left Spalding for Sleaford, thence to Billingborough in the road parcels van, to work the train back to Bourne and Spalding. Needing two sets of men for the one train did not contribute to the line's prosperity.

24.   Half a mile further on is the signal box at Four Cross Roads. It had a 12-lever frame and a gatewheel, with home and distant signals each way. Apart from breaking up the long section between Bourne East and Twenty, it was of importance because the M&GN provided water columns here. This was because Bourne was a GNR station and the M&GN were charged for using water there. The GN/M&GN boundary was marked by cast iron round plates fastened to the sleepers in the track on both sides of Bourne, which read "GNR".

TWENTY

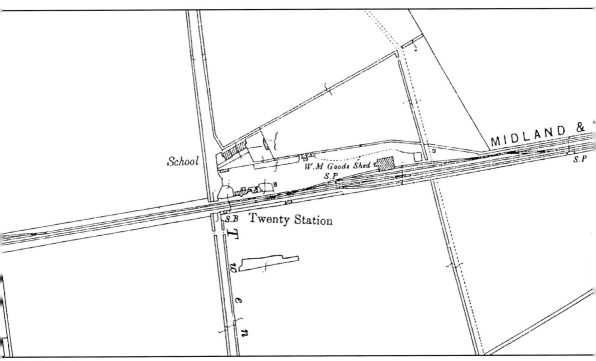

IX.   Seen in 1904 this station is not, contrary to popular opinion, named after a plot of land, but after the adjacent Twenty Lode, the name locally for fen waterways. On the left, the third line is the down refuge siding; the up refuge is the lower siding on the right. The goods shed was taken down in the late 1950s. Both this station and the next one at Counter Drain were closed between 9th October 1880 and 31st January 1881.

25.   Bourne Eau was a wide watercourse which had to be crossed on a quite substantial bridge, no. 229. This is the later down side, looking towards Twenty in May 1965. The original was constructed on cast iron piers, whereas this side has piers of concrete blocks. Very extensive reconstruction work took place in 1924, with single-line working and a temporary signal box installed.

TWENTY

PRIV

26. The down platform, was the original here before the line was doubled from Bourne; the small goods shed is beyond. On 2nd March 1959 the signal box had its instruments removed and was reduced to a points frame for the yard and siding connections, being released by the train staff. This view was taken on 9th October 1958. (L.Hails)

27. A matter of convenience! The unique, decorative cast iron gents urinal on the down platform is seen on 17th August 1960. It was the only one on the line and the lamp in front is also noteworthy.

28.   The up platform is seen from a stopping train on 27th May 1937. The M&GN had their own style of station nameboards made of concrete and were never "running-in boards" on this line. This signal box was opened on 5th June 1891, when the line was resignalled throughout as a through route by the Railway Signalling Co. The up starting signal, prominent by the box, was removed in the 1930s.

29.   We look towards Spalding from the down platform. The manual tablet receiving post for up trains is for some reason right at the far end, quite a long walk for the signalman when this was used. It is 17th August 1960 and the down line is not in use, the goods yard and up siding being connected to the former up line. The up siding was retained because a local farmer had built a loading dock for sugar beet at the end of it.

30. The station is seen from the Spalding end on 17th August 1960.

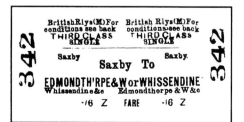

COUNTER DRAIN

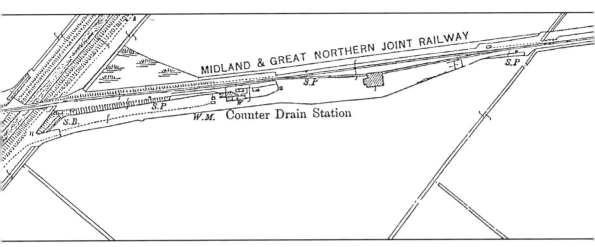

X.　　Another station named after a waterway, in this case the nearby "Drain" This map is from 1904, before the signal box was replaced by a gate cabin. The station was remote from the bridge owing to its gradients.

31.　　Continuing across the flat Fenland, we first cross the River Glen bridge and then, a short distance further on another bridge over the Counter Drain. This was reconstructed in the 1920s with the "X" shaped concrete structure. A signal box was provided on 8th June 1891, but was replaced by the hut built of concrete blocks that we see on the opposite side of the level crossing. This was done in 1924. The station house, in this case not actually at the station itself, is on the right. Seen on 17th August 1960, the bridge was still in situ in 2009.

32.   The long brick platform and station building is seen in typical Fen weather in December 1958. The crossing cabin is in the distance and there is a noticeable gradient up to the level crossing and river bridge, this being the reason for siting the platform where the track was more level. In the foreground is the rod to the down facing point into the goods yard siding and the 2-lever ground frame. This was the M&GN's pattern of the Midland Railway frame and was at this time released by the section tablet. (L.Hails)

33.   Turning round we see the goods yard and the more recent lock-up hut. This replaced the goods shed which had become unsafe and been demolished in 1925. The M&GN also had a distinctive style of concrete mileposts; the one for 5¼ is on the left.

NORTH DROVE

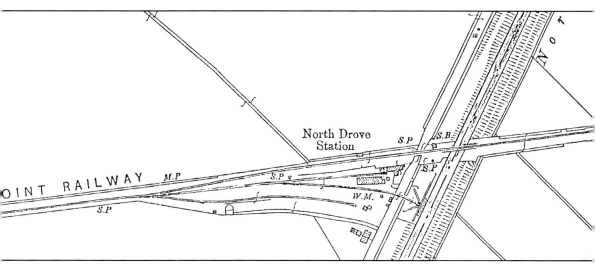

XI.   On to yet another fen name, a "Drove" being a rough track or road, in this case also next to the Drain of the same name. The station was sited here to provide an interchange for the barges, which once loaded and unloaded produce at the wharf. This was served by one of the yard sidings, which ran over the road and onto the wharf via a wagontable. This map is from 1904.

34.   We now approach the station and look at the goods yard from the Bourne end on 17th August 1960. The ground frame working the connection off the single line is behind us; originally this was the only one but on 2nd March 1959 another connection was installed facing from the Spalding direction, so that trains could call at the yard both outwards as well as returning. This can just be seen at the end of the platform; the Caution "C" board is for the relaying necessary.

35.   The wooden station building and goods yard are viewed from the adjacent road, after which the station was named. The Spalding Radial delivery lorry stands by the office. Parcels and small items were delivered over a wide area from Spalding Goods Depot, the local station yards only dealing with wagon load traffic. This yard was once extremely busy, the siding to the wharf already mentioned ran past the front of the weighbridge hut on the left. The goods yard closed on 30th March 1964.

36.   A train hauled by a 4MT 2-6-0 approaches the station in December 1958. The original brick platform on the right was replaced by the wooden platform on 19th August 1894, after a new bridge was constructed over the river. The crossing cabin on the right replaced the 1891 signal box opposite in August 1924.

37.   Looking along the line from the level crossing on 2nd August 1958, we can enjoy the station garden and rosebushes on the site of the original platform. The slew in the line needed in 1894 is evident, as is the emptiness of the Fen beyond. Also noticeable is the recent repainting of the waiting room. All the signal boxes and buildings were thus dealt with in the Summer, even though it was known that the line was to close for passengers! (D.Soggee)

38.   The line soon crosses the final Fen waterway, the South Drove Drain, and we take a look at the substantial girder bridge no. 216 reflected in the still waters of the Drain in May 1965. The level crossing of this name is on the right, with the gate cabin adjacent. The longer hut is a lamp and storeroom. The crossing house is out of sight on the right, having had to be rebuilt around 1924. The signal post seen was Cuckoo Junction down distant. The gate cabin was taken out of use on 28th February 1959, the level crossing gates being thereafter worked by the traincrew.

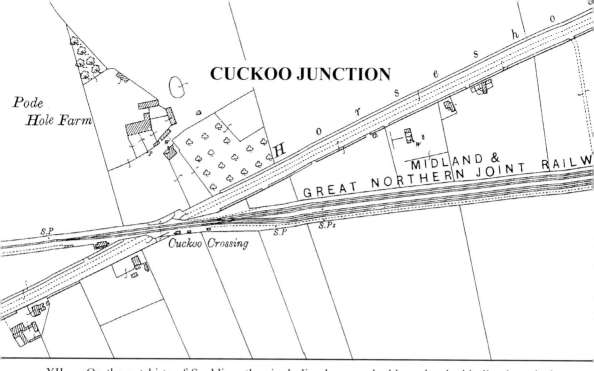

CUCKOO JUNCTION

Pode Hole Farm

MIDLAND & GREAT NORTHERN JOINT RAILW

Cuckoo Crossing

XII. On the outskirts of Spalding, the single line became double and a double line branched to the right, the avoiding line. The location is named after the Cuckoo Inn further back along the road.

39. The junction of the line to Spalding is on the left and onto the avoiding line on the right: the single line facing points are behind the photographer. This was a wide level crossing with large single gates to cover the angle of the road here and worked by a wheel in the signal box. This opened on 20th July 1891 and closed on 28th February 1959. Only the left-hand line remained in use from Spalding and the gates were operated by the traincrew. They are seen on 25th October 1958. (L.Hails)

40.   The junction of the two lines is seen from the signal box. Lifting has commenced of the down avoiding line, while the small hut down on the right remains in use. Spalding is seen in the distance.

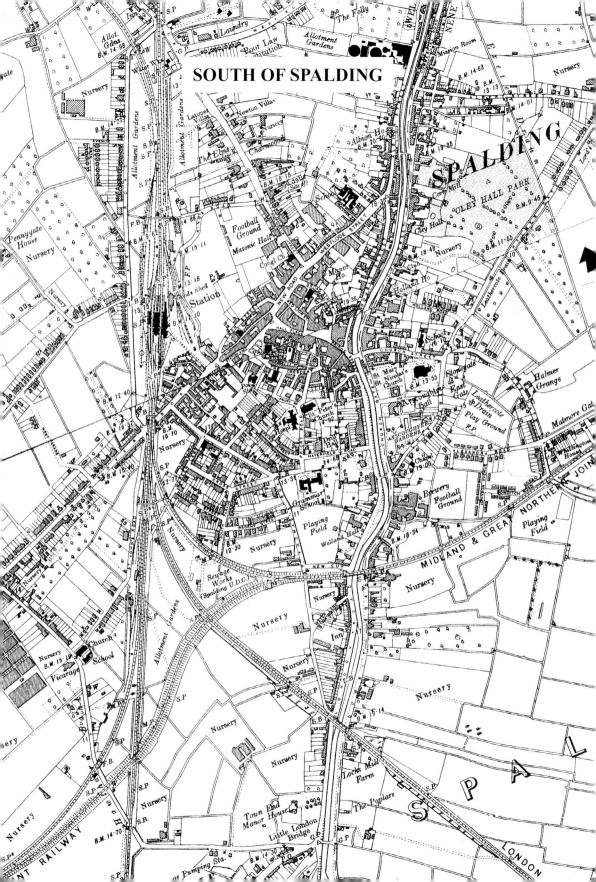

SOUTH OF SPALDING

43.   M&GN class C 4-4-0 no. 17 is seen in 1922. Posing are a group of cleaners, who doubtless would not have remained in this position for very long! This MR designed loco was built by Sharp Stewart in 1894.

44.   Looking smart, M&GN 4-4-0 no. 48 is in front of the original water tank in the 1930s. This locomotive was also built by Sharp Stewart, but in 1896.

41.   This is the M&GN's Hawthorn Bank no. 103 level crossing cabin and house. The provision of a footbridge here was required by the Board of Trade, this being a busy crossing even in the 1890s. This was also worked by the traincrew from 2nd March 1959. July 1960.

42.   The engine shed stands empty, having closed on 7th March 1960. On the left are the ashpit and coaling platform. The Midland Railway's goods shed is in the centre beyond, known as Spalding St. John's. The shunter poses in July 1960; the junction signals in the distance are for No. 1 box. A down train is signalled from the GN & GE line from March, to avoid the station platforms via the Western Goods line.

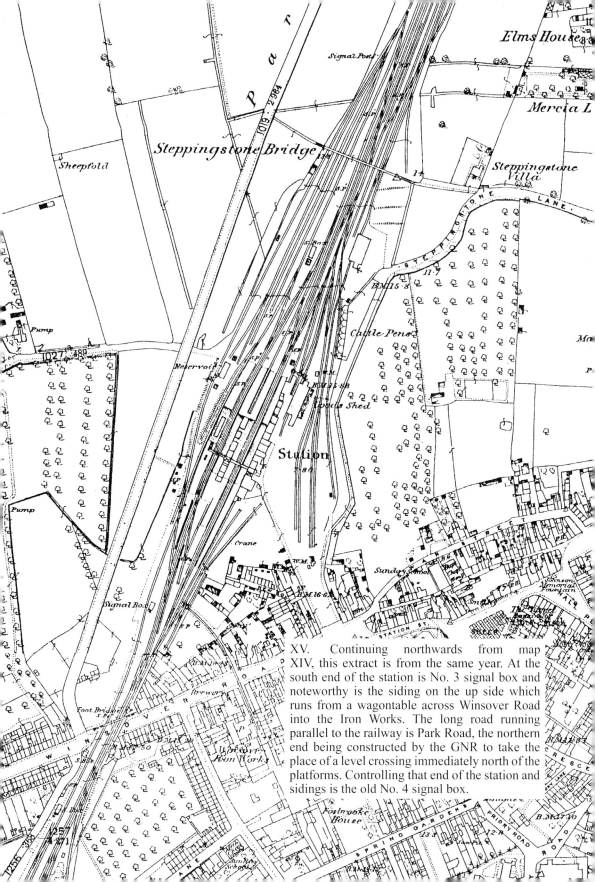

Elms House

Mercia L

Steppingstone Bridge

Sheepfold

Steppingstone Villa

Signal Post

14

BM·15·8

11·7

Pump

1027·480

Reservoir

Cattle Pens

Station

Goods Shed

Pump

Crane

Sunday School

Signal Box

Johnson Memorial Fountain

Footbridge

Iron Works

XV. Continuing northwards from map XIV, this extract is from the same year. At the south end of the station is No. 3 signal box and noteworthy is the siding on the up side which runs from a wagontable across Winsover Road into the Iron Works. The long road running parallel to the railway is Park Road, the northern end being constructed by the GNR to take the place of a level crossing immediately north of the platforms. Controlling that end of the station and sidings is the old No. 4 signal box.

← XIII.   The layout in 1932 is at 6ins to 1 mile. The two double-track lines from Cuckoo Junction are on the left, the lower being the avoiding line. This curves off towards the east, crossing over the GNR line from Peterborough and then over the GN&GE joint line from March, to join with the M&GN line from Spalding at Welland Bank. The other line from Cuckoo Junction heads to the north past first the M&GN locomotive shed, then the ex-MR goods shed and yard. The lines converge to pass over Winsover Road level crossing. At the northern end the GN&GE joint curves off to the left towards Lincoln and the ex-GNR continues north to Boston.

XIV.   The southern end of the layout shows the junctions in greater detail, it being dated before the two M&GN lines were doubled in 1893. The lower building alongside the single Bourne line is the engine shed; above it is the large MR goods shed. Green Lane footbridge has yet to be built. Near the junction, the lower signal box is the earlier No. 1 and No. 2 box is at the level crossing.

Foot Bridge

S.P.

S.P.

Foot Bridge

F.P.

St John the Baptist's Church

School

S.P.

Signal Post

Signal Post

Port

Port

Port

Port

Port

Port

GREAT NORTHERN & GR

45.   On the same date another engine is pictured outside the shed, this time 0-6-0 no. 86. This class J4 was constructed by Dübs & Co in 1901.

46.   Here we have 0-6-0 no. 4120, this time in LNER days. It was construced in 1899 by Dübs & Co. and became class J4.

SPALDING

→ 48. On the same day, we view the junctions at the south of the station, from the footbridge. Below are the double sets of gates at Winsover Road, known locally as the Eight Gates. To ease the work of the signalman at this busy box these were power-operated. On the left is the double track of the line towards Sutton Bridge and next on the left is the GN&GE joint line from March. The GN line from Peterborough is straight ahead, and next to it is the line to Bourne. This was singled as from 2nd March 1959 and wide-to-gauge single line facing points are in the distance. St. John's goods yard is on the right, with the loco shed beyond.

47. In July 1960 all the local station masters were directed to attend a re-railing exercise in St. John's goods yard. A K2 locomotive and some wagons were provided and one was put off the road.

49. Turning round we see the south end of the station. To the extreme left is the turntable, the local gas wagon being parked on it. Beyond this the western goods line heads off round the back of the station and sidings. Then there is the engine line and the outer face of the west island platform; this is the Bourne line. In between this and the centre island platform run the down joint and down main lines. Continuing to the right are the up joint and up main platforms. Finally, on the far →

right are the up bay and the flower sidings. The old No. 3 signal box had stood in the centre, next to the buffer stop. A quirk of the layout was that trains from Bourne could only run in to the down joint platform, via the long crossover. Trains to Bourne had to be drawn forward at the far end of the station and shunted back into the Bourne line. Trains from Bourne for Sutton Bridge had to proceed via the crossovers to gain the up main line at the bottom right hand corner.

50.   Here we see the shunting as explained in the previous caption. The final up "Leicester" from the east has arrived in the up joint platform, hauled by an Ivatt 4MT 2-6-0. J. Barker's "Thats Yer Lot" poster has been brought across from the incoming engine, and the driver of no. 43060 is fastening it to the front of the replacement engine. The left-hand signal is off for the whole train, complete with passengers, to be drawn down the eastern goods line to the left of the white-painted cabin and No. 2 signal box by the footbridge in the distance. We see the shunter kneeling down, clamping the first set of points which will become facing to the train when being set back. The station inspector looks to be walking across to supervise the movement. When the train is drawn right down, the second set of points will be clamped as well, as neither have any facing point locks fitted. The down yard sidings are on the left and the up yard on the right. We note the old GNR somersault signals were still in use on 28th February 1959. (J.Langford)

WELLAND BANK

51.   When GNR trains were running into Spalding via the line to the right and Midland Railway trains over the avoiding line to the left, this was an important junction. After trains were diverted to run into Spalding and out again, the use of the avoiding line decreased. Latterly its main use was for turning engines. For the opening of the avoiding line a separate signal box was provided on the extreme left of the picture. It was soon realised, however, that this was not necessary and Duck Hall was closed as early as 16th March 1897. The junction is seen in May 1961.

52.   We now turn round and look eastwards towards the signal box and footbridge on the same date. There was quite a climb up to here out of Spalding; the crossover in front of us is the one used for engines to set back, to reverse round the avoiding line. As there was no down starting signal provided ahead of the box, all such movements had first to be checked at the home signal seen in the distance in the previous photograph, then a move forward, not an easy job for the driver.

53.   A replacement signal box opened in 1892 for the building of the avoiding line. Some contemporary advertising for local firms is on offer. Also of note is the swan-neck gas lamp on the left and another for illumination on the footbridge in May 1961.

54.   The large girder bridge over the River Welland was provided for the doubling of the line into Spalding, which opened on 26th March 1893. The level crossing gates were worked by a wheel in the signal box. On the far bank is Cowbit Road level crossing and the gate box of that name can just be glimpsed on the other side. The signals are the junction up homes, towards Cuckoo Junction and Spalding No. 1 respectively. The first signal box, then named Water Lane, stood on the far side of the nearest level crossing, but had to be replaced because it was in the way of the up side of the new bridge seen in May 1961.

CLAY LAKE

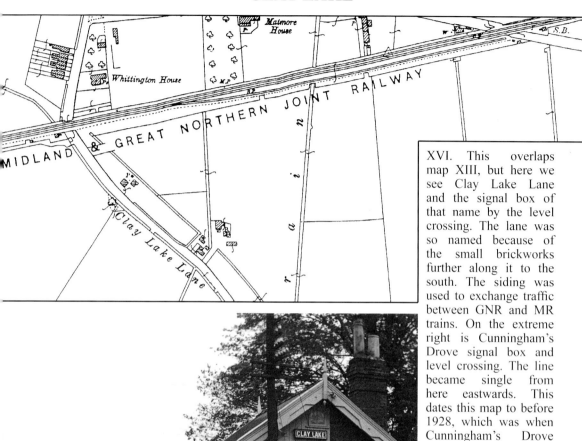

XVI. This overlaps map XIII, but here we see Clay Lake Lane and the signal box of that name by the level crossing. The lane was so named because of the small brickworks further along it to the south. The siding was used to exchange traffic between GNR and MR trains. On the extreme right is Cunningham's Drove signal box and level crossing. The line became single from here eastwards. This dates this map to before 1928, which was when Cunningham's Drove box was closed.

55.   Here is the sturdy brick signal box and level crossing looking towards Sutton Bridge in July 1960. This was opened on 17th March 1896, ready for the doubling from Welland Bank on 19th April 1896. It was one of the few signal boxes which remained staffed after 28th February 1959. This section of the line into Spalding was singled on 1st April 1964 and it was then reduced to a gate box.

56.   The M&GN also had colour light signals and was progressive in that it carried out its own rationalisation schemes. In September 1932 the nearby signal box at Cunningham's Drove was closed, the crossing gates there being controlled by a ground frame released by Clay Lake. This early scheme resulted in the new signal having splitting junction distant signals for Welland Bank, next along the line. The upper lens is the up home and shows red or green. The two lower aspects on either side show yellow or green, indicating whether the junction ahead is set for the avoiding line or Spalding. The board on the post behind refers to a telephone instruction. On the left is the up traffic siding in July 1960.

57.   Cunningham's Drove Gatehouse no. 100 and crossing cabin are seen on 5th November 1960, looking east towards the Coronation Channel river bridge. This was a new cut as part of the flood relief scheme to provide an alternative route for the River Welland round the outside of Spalding. On 20th August 1951, the main line was relaid to the right of the track seen here and the level of the old line gradually raised up to the level of the new river bridge that was to be built. On 25th November 1952, the new bridge was brought into use and the lines diverted onto it. Cunningham's Drove signal box was down on the right, at the former lower level.

58.   This photograph shows the single line facing points, worked by a point motor, an arrangement again dating from September 1932. Its battery cases are on the right. Since the line has been raised to clear the river bridge just behind us, the level crossing gates at Cunningham's Drove do not meet across the line owing to the angle of the road. This is July 1960.

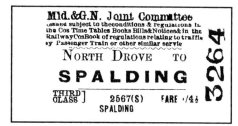

Mld.&G.N. Joint Committee
Issued subject to the conditions & regulations in the Cos Time Tables Books Bills&Notices& in the Railway CosBook of regulations relating to traffic by Passenger Train or other similar servic

NORTH DROVE   TO

SPALDING

THIRD CLASS]   2567(S)   FARE ·/4½
SPALDING

3264

British Railways (E)   British Railways (E)
ONE PRAM or   ONE PRAM or
CHILD'S MAIL CT   CHILD'S MAIL CT
Accomp'g Passenger   Accomp'g Passenger
At Owner's Risk   At Owner's Risk

Any Station not   NORTH DROVE
exceeding 5 miles   TO Any Station not
distant TO   exceeding 5 miles
NORTH DROVE   distant
Rate 0/9   Rate 0/9
For conditions see over   For conditions see over

0326   0326

WESTON

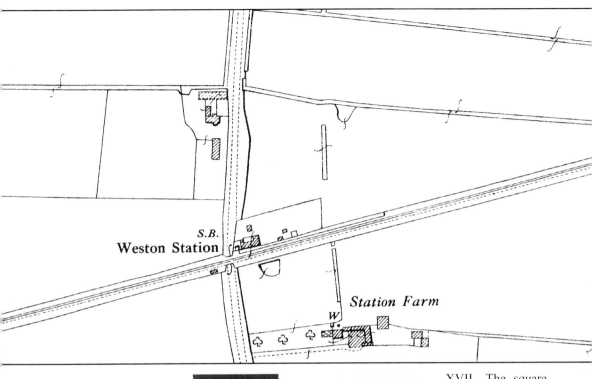

S.B.
Weston Station

Station Farm

W

XVII. The square of land shown on this 1932 map in which the station building stands was intended for a goods yard, should one be needed, but nothing was ever provided.

59. M&GN hardware included this unusually worded trespasser notice near no. 98 crossing. The only similar one known is on the Peterborough to Wisbech line, near Wisbech St. Mary. The photograph is from 5th November 1960.

60.   This is the substantial station building; the original seems to be a modification of the usual gatehouses along the line. At a later date a slightly taller extension was added, at right angles to the track. Subsequently another extension was provided at the rear and a urinal at the righthand end. Hidden by the nearside wicket gate late in 1958 is a small ground frame for the up and down level crossing distant signals. (L.Hails)

61.   Note the unusual station name set into the brickwork of the building. This is the only known example on the whole line and the reason for it is not apparent.

62.   The platform was unusually lengthy for such a small station in a sparsely populated area, the village of Weston being a mile away. This view on 5th November 1960 is looking back towards Spalding and the goods yard was to be on the right. This did not escape the notice of local farmers, who petitioned the M&GN for facilities. It was decided on 24th September 1895, however, not to proceed and the farmers were told to take their produce to Moulton.

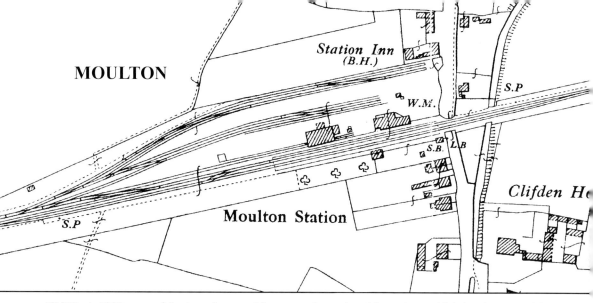

MOULTON

XVIII. A 1932 map of the long loop and large goods yard at this station, which by the turn of the century, was inadequate for the traffic handled. Crossovers were situated in the sidings to enable wagons to be run round. East of the level crossing, the line crosses over the old Moulton River. The scale is 25 ins to 1 mile.

63. The station layout is seen looking east on 5th November 1960. The goods yard was quite large, but was still in full use right up to the final closure with a large outwards traffic in agricultural implements and trailers. This was a local industry, but shunting for up trains posed problems, as there was only the connection from the yard out onto the down main. This is seen in the middle distance and necessitated up trains having to run round and then draw forward. The area on the right was for up sidings which were never laid.

64.   To assist with the traffic a very old mobile crane was provided. Its somewhat fragile jib has a chain instead of a wire rope and it is fitted with cast iron spoked wheels. Rolling stock enthusiasts will notice the once common variety of wagons in the background on 5th November 1960.

65.   Here we stand on the end of the down platform and look back towards Spalding. In the far distance is no. 95 crossing. Typical M&GN fencing is at the rear of the platform and the much used crossover is on the left. There is a nice platform lamp and more items of rolling stock in the yard on 5th November 1960.

66.   Flower traffic boomed in the 1960s, with the introduction of a per box rate to compete with (and under-cut) road transport; up to then it had been charged on a weight basis. But there were still large quantities handled before that, as this picture from around 1925 shows. What is unusual is that these are on the down platform, whereas most was forwarded to the west from the up side. The large goods shed is seen to advantage.

67.   The station building and platforms are seen late in 1958, looking towards Holbeach with no. 94 crossing in the distance. The station master here at the time was the appropriately named Mr. Moulton. The signal box was opened, as a replacement, on 15th March 1899, then at the Spalding end of the up platform. To achieve economy in controlling the level crossing, it was moved to the site seen here in around July 1926. (L.Hails)

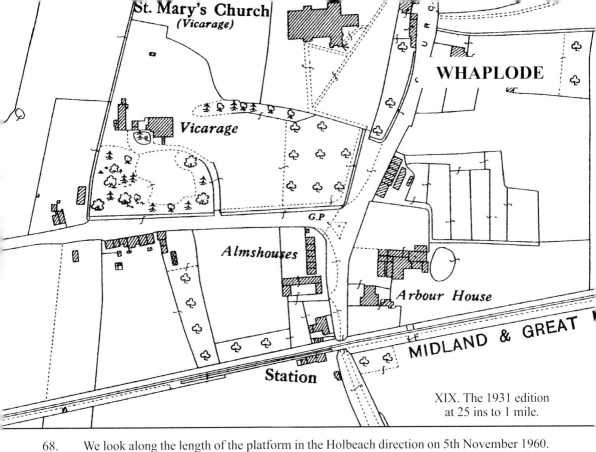

St. Mary's Church
(Vicarage)

WHAPLODE

Vicarage

G.P

Almshouses

Arbour House

MIDLAND & GREAT

Station

XIX. The 1931 edition
at 25 ins to 1 mile.

68.   We look along the length of the platform in the Holbeach direction on 5th November 1960. M&GN fencing is at the rear and the goods yard was to be on the other side of this, on the right. To this end a full size signal box was provided on 31st July 1891, even with locking in the frame for the siding connection. Local farmers here also sent a petition to the M&GN and again it was decided on 3rd November 1896, that other joint stations were nearby; Moulton was two miles away and Holbeach nearly five. Another petition was presented, but the reply on 24th April 1911 was the same and the yard was never built.

69.   The station building was in the same style as the level crossing houses on the line, but was never extended. The urinal beyond is more modern. Just to the left is the 5-lever ground frame for the distant signals; it replaced the signal box in the early 1920s. In the fruit and flower season all the barrows along the platform were in full use. The poster on the end of the building in late 1958 announces that Mr Moulton is here to serve you, this station coming under him at Moulton. These posters incidentally, at stations all along the line, caused much merriment, as the term used meant something different in the livestock industry! Next to the poster hangs one type of M&GN Telegraph Board, with an oval top. The reverse was black and if it was turned round it indicated to a passing lineman that the electrical equipment was out of order. (L.Hails)

70.   Returning to 5th November 1960, the leading porter poses proudly for the photographer. The site of the signal box is immediately on the left.

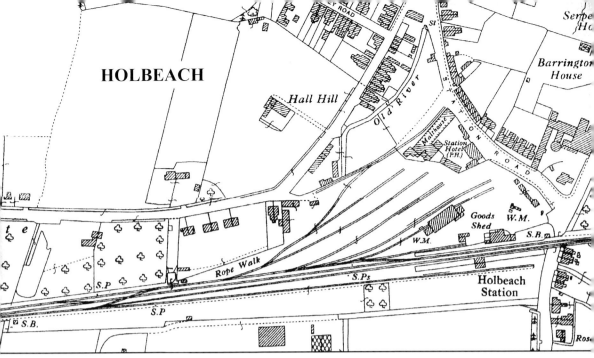

HOLBEACH

XX.   Construction of the sidings required the old Holbeach River to be covered over, to the chagrin of the Drainage Board. The Rope Walk on this 1932 map at 20ins to 1 mile, had to be resited when the yard was expanded. The northernmost siding served the malthouse and other premises and was known as the Tramway. There are two weighing machines, the one at the end of the goods shed being for wagons.

71.   The station is seen from the Spalding end on 10th February 1962, with the West signal box on the right: this opened on 10th May 1891. We are standing on the down facing points and the line to the left is the long shunting siding. The station is in the distance.

72.	Unique on the M&GN was this collapsible tablet catcher, although there was a slightly different delivery one at Sheringham West. It is designed that the impact of a passing train throws it backwards into the box on the right, where it is held down by a sprung catch. Seen in April 1961, it was pulled up into position by a wire from the signal box, there being a grip in the floor at the end of the lever frame. This was unfortunately the cause of a fatal accident in January 1913. A permanent way sub-inspector was trying to alight from a slowly moving train, when the catcher arm rebounded upwards again because the impact was insufficient to engage the catch. He was conveyed to Spalding on a hastily arranged special train, but sadly died soon after admission. This design of apparatus, as with the whole Whittaker system, came from the Somerset & Dorset joint line.

73.	This is another view of the large goods yard, seen from West signal box in April 1961. Bushes on the left cover the site of the old ropewalk and the miniature somersault signal is off for a shunting movement out of the yard. The up refuge siding is on the right; trains which needed to shunt in the yard were placed in this to clear the main line.

74.   The East or Station signal box, also opened on 10th May 1891, when the long crossing
loop was provided. The fine right-hand bracket signal is the down starter, with the distant for no. 91
crossing in the distance. Beyond the single line facing points is the up home signal, with the West box
distant below. The signalman is seen watching for an up freight train to appear round the corner.

75.   The platforms with the station building and east box beside the level crossing are seen in November 1961. On the left in the yard are the weighbridge and merchants huts. When the line opened there was a small engine shed here, this being initially a terminus. It was on the site of the up platform on the right. Unlike other such stations, the up platform waiting room has an extended awning, supported on posts.

FLEET

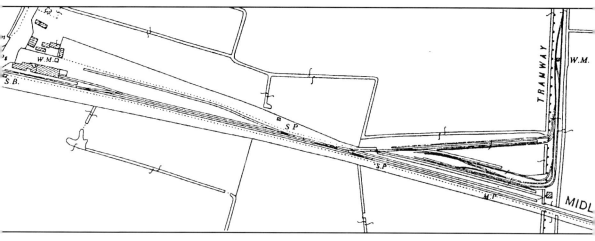

XXI.   This map is dated after 1909 as it includes the narrow gauge lines. Standard gauge sidings ran on both sides of the dock and also alongside the light railway tracks in the private yard.

76.   The station was recorded in around 1925, with the clerk looking out of the office door and the large goods shed at the far end of the platform. The signal box casts its shadow across the scene and the black painted hut on the right contains a ground frame which worked, remotely by wire, Clayton Fogging Machines at the up and down distants.

77. At around the same time, an up express goods runs through and is seen from the signal box. It appears to be hauled by an M&GN class DA 0-6-0 and we note the length of the train.

78. We have already mentioned the heavy fruit and flower traffic in the 1930s and here is another example. This is the 5pm fruit train, Long Sutton to Saxby, after having picked up at this station. The engine is way in the distance, the rear being brought up by an LMS brake van.

79. An action shot, also from the 1930s, was taken in the split-second of tablets being exchanged by hand on a down express. The signalman, complete with uniform hat, stands on the platform and the fireman leans from the cab, the driver glancing back to ensure that all is well. The up starter, seen above the engine, has the lamp mounted lower than the arm. Both this and the down home in the rear are GNR somersault signals.

80. An interesting comparison with the previous shot of the station, is from late in 1958. Noticeable is the removal of the advertisement boards and the lack of platform seats. At most stations they were removed at the 1959 closure. There are now only a few vans in the yard and the fogging hut has gone. Maybe this happened when the signal box closed on 3rd November 1957, after which the distant signals and yard points were worked by ground frames.

81. The local coal merchants are unloading a wagon in the yard onto their then new motor lorry, in the 1930s. The coalman surveys the photographer, as his assistant pauses whilst shovelling loose coal into the sacks.

82. Whilst loading fruit in the goods yard in the 1920s, the merchant proudly displays his punnet of strawberries to the photographer, in front of his then also new car. Behind him is a wagon load of the same fruit.

83. Around December 1909, a local farmer, constructed a system of 2ft gauge light railways from his, and other farms, out in the Fen, to bring his produce to the railway. These terminated in a large dock, with standard gauge sidings on each side and there were also similar exchange sidings down below on the level. This is the scene from the dock, with a narrow gauge track along the edge. Another ends at a buffer stop in the centre. The course of the narrow gauge line curves round to the left, where the weighbridge hut is situated. Gedney church is on the horizon and is seen in the 1950s.

84. This is the arrangement of tracks at the weighbridge hut, in the 1930s. There was not so much traffic at the time, although there was a brief revival during the war in 1939-45.

GEDNEY

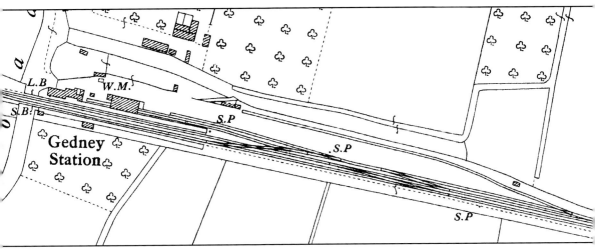

XXII. Not such a long loop as it seems, as the east end facing points are actually in-between the two crossovers into the yard sidings. The uppermost line on the right is the shunting spur, and down trains had to set back out of this into the platform line, before re-starting for the east. This map is dated 1931, so it is after the signal box was moved in about December 1925 from the east end of the platform to be next to the level crossing. The scale is 25 ins to 1 mile.

85.   The level crossing gates are open for us to get a good view of the station and goods yard seen on 18th July 1961. In readiness for provision of a loop here the signal box was opened on 29th March 1897.

← 86. Here is a closer view of the down side station buildng and the large goods shed in about 1959. A train is shunting at the west end of the yard, having left its brake van on the down main line. It is noticeable that the down platform has been extended since the early N&S days. At some stage a replacement gate has been fitted. The one on the left is the M&GN original, with upright rods and diamond pattern target. The gate on the right has an LNER circular target. (L.Hails)

↙ 87. Staff recover in the signal box from snow clearing early in 1959, when "Wellies" are mandatory.

88.   This is a view of the goods yard seen from the end of the up platform. The crossover nearest to us leads over into the down siding and the down main facing points are beyond. The line continued as a shunting siding almost as far as the trees in the distance. It is 10th June 1960 and not the season for loading sugar beet. The two set-back discs down on the left are of two different types, an old GNR revolving disc in front of a later LNER/BR type behind. In the centre is the tall down advance starter, which has had the arm replaced with an upper-quadrant type. The lower miniature arm for the the down siding is the older GNR somersault type.

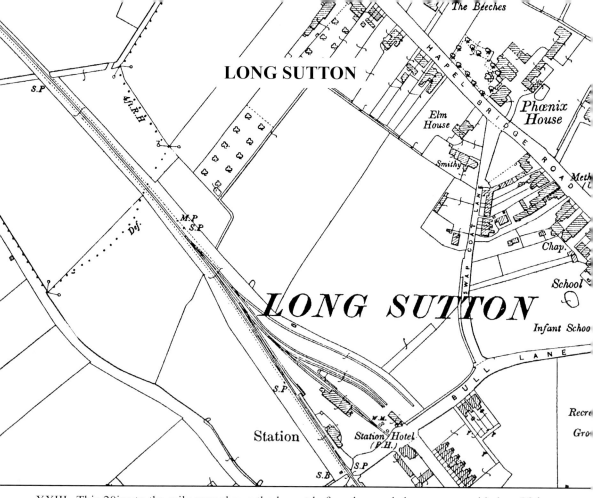

XXIII. This 20ins to the mile map shows the layout before the goods loop was provided on 30th September 1911. The large goods shed and equally large loading dock indicate the amount of traffic handled here. The building near to the weighing machine was the stables, for the shunting and dray horses. Of historical interest is Swapcoat Lane, named supposedly after the outlaw Dick Turpin, being where he changed his clothes before his ride to York.

89.   A real gem to survive, this is the earliest known photograph of the station. It must be soon after opening as the house is not yet built. In the background is the Station Hotel; this has outlived the station and is still there in 2008.

90.   As a contrast, here is another early picture, but now we see the house and office. Traces can be seen of what was there originally. This is certainly before the goods loop was provided. There are many advertisements and poster boards, maybe it is the station master on the right.

91.   It was not true that DMUs were not used on the line. Albeit on an excursion, here are two Cravens units running through the platform on 13th August 1958. This train conveyed a party from Boston to Hunstanton.

92.　　In happier times the last Sunday excursion to Hunstanton was on 14th September 1958 and class 4MT no. 43085 heads eight coaches into the short platform. These trains were generally well supported and this one will have to draw up. The station gong is prominent on the left, with the yard ground frame cabin beyond. The large station house, in which the author lived at the time, is on the right.

93.　　Here is the scene just before the closure and we see a lot of further adaptation, mostly in the doors and windows, but now the booking office is the one with the door open in the centre and at this end there is the goods office, with the door on the other side. Next to the barrow and covered weighing machine on the right, is the fish dock, kept separate for obvious reasons. The shadow is from the signal box behind the photographer. On the wall is another of the "here to serve you" notices, in this case Mr E.L.Back, the author's father. (L.Hails)

Last passengers

To mark this sad event, we close with a grand finale of the photographs taken on the last day, 28th February 1959 and just before, by Long Sutton station master Mr. E.L.Back M.B.E.

94. On the day previous the station staff posed outside the goods office for the last time.

95. The die is cast. In place of the usual timetable posters we see the closure notices.

96.	The line from Spalding was within the Cambridge district, but from 2nd March 1959 it was transferred to Lincoln. The Cambridge officials were well respected and on the final Friday afternoon they visited stations along the line to say goodbye to their staff. Standing on the end of the platform is the inspector, on the right, next to him is the district operating superintendent. Next is signalman and then the district inspector. The double set of level crossing gates in the background was provided for an up line which was never laid.

From the left: "Jimmy" Greeves, H.S.Crosthwaite, L. Bingham and F. Goward.

97.	It is not generally known that J. Barker prepared two "Thats Yer Lot" posters. One was for the up and down Leicester expresses and the second was attached to the morning goods train to Spalding. It is here in the yard with the crew posing on 28th February 1959.

98.　　The last through down goods was the 1.58pm from Spalding to South Lynn class J pickup. This approaches the yard hauled by class J6 0-6-0 no. 64278 on 28th February 1959.

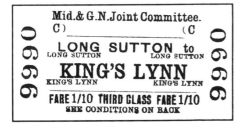

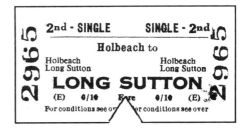

99.   Another last and this is the final up Leicester passing through at speed with the "Thats yer Lot" poster on the front. This is the 9.02am from Yarmouth, hauled by class 4MT no. 43161.

100.   The 9.55am Saxby to Kings Lynn approaches the down home signal. It is headed by class J6 no. 64172 and heads watch out of the coach windows for the last time.

101.   Later in the afternoon the final down "Leicester" approaches the same spot, this being the 1.45pm Birmingham to Yarmouth. The outward engine, class 4MT no. 43161, came off the up working at Spalding and waited to take over this return train.

102.   This is the last up passenger train of all, the 4.20pm Kings Lynn to Nottingham. The ubiquitous 4MT no. 43091 is running tender-first as it leaves the station. This train had another South Lynn crew.

2175 X
This cancels handbill D2087X

GREAT NORTHERN

DAY EXCURSIONS

TO

NOTTINGHAM

EVERY
WEDNESDAY FRIDAY and SATURDAY
SEPTEMBER 17th 1958
until further notice
(EXCEPT DECEMBER 24th 26th 27th MARCH 27th 28th MAY 16th)

OUTWARD JOURNEY			RETURN FARES SECOND CLASS	RETURN JOURNEY			
		a.m.	s. d.			p.m.	p.m.
Spalding (Town) ...	dep.	8 27	10/9	Nottingham (Midland) ...	dep.	4 20	7 45
Counter Drain ...	"	8 36	9/9	Edmondthorpe and Wymondham ...	arr.	5 22	—
Twenty	"	8 40	9/6	South Witham	"	5 32	8 43
Bourne	"	8 49	8/9	Castle Bytham	"	5 42	8 52
Castle Bytham	"	9 10	7/3	Bourne	"	5 53	9 4
South Witham	"	9 21	6/3	Twenty	"	6 6	9 12
Edmondthorpe and Wymondham ...	"	9 30	5/3	Counter Drain ...	"	6 10	9 16
Nottingham (Midland)	arr.	10 25		Spalding (Town) ...	"	6 19	9 26

PASSENGERS RETURN ON DAY OF ISSUE ONLY AS SHOWN ABOVE

Tickets can be obtained IN ADVANCE at stations or the following travel agency

Spalding Travel Agency ... ... Dembleby House, Broad Street, Spalding

Further information will be supplied on application to stations, offices, travel agencies or to Traffic Manager, 26/28 Newland, Lincoln (Tel : Lincoln 11352)

CONDITIONS OF ISSUE

These tickets are issued subject to the British Transport Commission's published Regulations and Conditions applicable to British Railways exhibited at their stations or obtainable free of charge at station booking offices

LUGGAGE ALLOWANCES are as set out in these general notices

CHILDREN under three years of age, free ; three years and under fourteen, half-fares

London, October 1958

Published by British Railways (Eastern Region) Printed in Great Britain 1448/10/58

103.   We now revert to the previous evening for the opportunity to see one of the M&GN's crack express freights on its final night. This was the 12.40pm from Lowestoft Central, known as *The Fish*. Out of the darkness, running at speed, hurtles class J6 no. 64278. There is a small light on the end of the signal box behind us. The signalman holds up the large pouch, shining his oil handlamp on it. The fireman crouches down in the cab throwing off the tablet for the section they are leaving. The guard waved goodbye to us as the brake van went past on 27th February 1959.

104. Back to the last night, the final passenger train of all is at the platform. This is the 4.20pm Nottingham to Kings Lynn, with class 4MT no. 43091.

105. And so to the end. Up in the signal box we see in the foreground the Midland Railway lever frame, with the gatewheel at the end. Signalman Len Bingham is operating the Tyers no. 6 type tablet instrument, receiving train out of section for the last train, seen in picture 119. He turned the commutator to the right, pushed home the slide and sent the 7-5-5 bell signal. Closing the signal box he turned to us and quietly said "That's it, then".

106.   The M&GN Preservation Society ran a special along the branch on 27th May 1961, one of several lines visited that day. It was hauled by class 4MT no. 43151, specially cleaned for the occasion with whitened buffers. It is passing the goods yard and was the longest train seen for years. It carries a large square headboard on the tender. On the front was a large circular one to match the round boiler.

Goods only

107.   The first train from Spalding after the closure to passengers was the 8.30am class K to Sutton Bridge. Here we see Ivatt 2-6-0 no. 43060, on 2nd March 1959. It is aproaching the down home signal with no. 85 gates in the rear. Culvert 185 goes under the line at this point, marked by the usual M&GN number disc.

108.   The author spent much time at this station and this gives us the opportunity to see the variety of trains and traction that travelled the line at various times. On 11th June 1959 a Matisa self-propelled track recorder gauged the line. We see it approaching the down home signal.

109. To cater for the afternoon traffic there were two trains leaving the yard. Here is the coal yard on the left and the goods yard over on the right in June 1959. On the left is the 4.45pm Class C parcels train to Kings Cross. The correct headcode has not yet been put into place and there is a brake van at the leading end because the engine had to run round at Spalding. On this occasion a grimy 4MT has been provided by the Boston locomotive foreman. On the right are the vans →

110. Although provided at every station, photographs of weighbridges are comparatively rare. This is the 20 ton one, with its neat little hut. It was in frequent use, as the local coal merchants in the yard often weighed complete lorry loads. The charge was 3d per ton, minimum 1s. 0d, and a ticket for this was written out every time by the goods porter. M&GN fencing is in the rear and the lamp room is on the extreme right. The large yard had three entrances; the centre gate is on the left with the Station Hotel behind. The notice on the end is an LNER example.

which will form the 5.15 class J departure. The afternoon down train from Spalding has run through to Sutton Bridge and will return at 4.15. It will then shunt here as required and couple up its existing load to the vans that we see. Loading is in progress, with several vehicles from growers and agents, plus the road motor from Sutton Bridge, which has collected traffic from the agency at Tydd, established there after 28th February 1959.

111. Another trial was held with a 204hp diesel on 19th April 1960. Here is Drewry D2024, which managed to get as far as here, allegedly after having to leave half of its train at Holbeach yet still taking nearly twice as long to get here. It was not seen here again.

112.   On 10th July 1961, class 4MT locomotive no. 43143 enters the station on the main line with a weedkiller train. On the left is the goods loop, which was bi-directional. On the right is the yard spur.

➔ 113.   The station gardens won many prizes annually in the regional competition. Laid out as flower beds and narrow lawns by the station master, with the assistance of some of the staff in their spare time, they received many visitors. This is one on the up side in the summer of 1961. We also see the points into the goods yard in the centre, with the whitewashed permanent way hut beyond.

➔ 114.   A classic shot of a typical train of the time, on 31st August 1961. As was often the case, the 350hp locomotive, class 10 DE no. D3490, has a maximum load, mostly timber for Travis & Arnold at Sutton Bridge, which will have to be first placed in the adjacent loop to enable the rest of the train to be shunted. The points at the far end were worked by the ground frame cabin, seen in the distance. This necessitated teamwork, for shunting the curved sidings really needed three men, one to work the gound frame, one for the uncoupling and another for the point levers into the sidings. But the 1959 staffing meant that there were only two, the guard and the foreman. Timber traffic was abundant and often some had to be left behind at Spalding for the followng day.

115.   Traction on the branch was the subject of discussion at "high level", but use of a 204hp locomotive failed dismally because of the huge loads involved. Next came the trial of D3626 on 8th December 1959 and this time, although limited to 20mph, it was a success. The 350hp locomotives were rostered as from 25th January 1960 and thereafter shared duties with the 4MTs. Indeed quite often trains were loaded up to the limit of the diesel locomotives and here we see a typical example. D3442 heads back to Spalding on 29th May 1962, with the 5-15pm class J train. The spire of Long Sutton church rises over the trees.

116. Any engine could turn up to work the 4.45 Kings Cross parcels, depending on what power was available. A great surprise, however, in November 1962 was class B1 4-6-0 no. 61059. It has propelled its brake van outwards from Spalding for this working and now stands ready for departure, tender-first. There were no complaints of lack of power on that day!

117. Here we see the approach to the yard, with the station in the distance in October 1964. The main arm is the down home and the miniature applies to the goods loop on the right. The yard shunting siding ends on the left.

118.   It is time to look at the renowned workhorse of the latter days of the M&GN route, the Ivatt 4MT 2-6-0. Never referred to as "Flying Pigs", the M&GN footplate staff took them to their hearts. Here is no. 43092 on 26th October 1964.

119.   It is 2nd April 1965. A sad day as this is the last train along the line. By various means traffic had been driven away and here is D3442 ready to leave for Spalding. None of this is revenue earning. The train is clearing the rest of the stock, some eight vans and two brakes. The signal box was in use until the end. The ploughed remains of the prize winning gardens are on the right and the station gong was silent for ever.

120.   The final shot of the line is from 10th January 1960 and is of the renowned "Pop Bottle Bridge", no. 183, a mile further east towards Sutton Bridge. It was the only one from west of Bourne to South Lynn, and the reason for building such a grandiose structure, with room for a double line, is not known, particularly in such a flat area and with the original company in financial straits. Most of the soil for the steep inclines on either side was dug out of a pit on the left. The name is because an old fashioned glass pop bottle was cemented into the wing wall on the far side with its end outwards. The bridge is still there to this day.

For other photographs of this station, please see
Peterborough to Kings Lynn **and** ***Branch Lines around Wisbech,***
both Middleton Press albums.

MP Middleton Press

EVOLVING THE ULTIMATE RAIL ENCYCLOPEDIA

Easebourne Lane, Midhurst, West Sussex.
GU29 9AZ Tel:01730 813169

www.middletonpress.co.uk   email:info@middletonpress.co.uk
A-978 0 906520 B- 978 1 873793 C- 978 1 901706 D-978 1 904474 E- 978 1 906008

OOP Out of print at time of printing - Please check availability BROCHURE AVAILABLE SHOWING NEW TITLES